TON

DOUBLE
DANGER

Midori looked out of the window of the British Airways jumbo jet. It was nearly dark. She could see the lights of Heathrow Airport down below. This was her last view of England, her home for the past six months.

She sat back in her seat and closed her eyes. She thought about her English lessons. She thought about her new friends. She thought about her home-stay family, the Jacksons. She thought about David Jackson, her friend.

The flight attendant brought Midori a glass of orange juice. She had a long journey ahead of her. First there was an eleven-hour flight to Tokyo. Then she had to change airports and catch a plane to Fukuoka. Fukuoka - home!

Midori took out the last letter from her mother. 'You'll see us as soon as you come out of the Customs Hall.' Midori smiled.

She put the letter back in her bag. A photo fell out. It was a photo of David. Suddenly, Midori's thoughts were back in England.

Midori pushed her trolley through the Customs Hall. Her mother, father and brother were all there. They looked very excited.

Midori waved. 'Hello, everyone,' she said. 'I'm glad to be back.'

On the way home, Midori told her family all about her stay in England.

'You remember everything,' her father smiled. 'I'm sure you've got enough stories for a year. You never forget anything, do you?'

They arrived home. During dinner, the phone rang. It was David.

'Hello, Midori,' he said. 'Guess what? My father's coming to Tokyo on business and I'm coming with him. Can I come to Fukuoka and visit you?'

'What good news!' Midori said. 'First I must ask my father. Wait for my call.'

When Midori asked her father about David, he smiled.

'David's family were very kind to you in England,' he said. 'Of course he can visit us. He's very welcome. I'm looking forward to meeting him.'

Midori was very excited. 'Thank you, Dad,' she said.

She phoned David and told him the news.

Two weeks later, David arrived at Hakata station on the Bullet Train from Tokyo. Midori and her father were at the station to meet him.

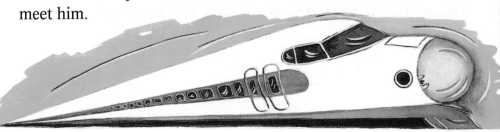

'Hello, David,' Midori said. 'I'm so pleased to see you. This is my father.'

'How do you do, sir?' said David.

'How do you do, David? Welcome to Japan.'

Midori's father looked carefully at David. Then he said, 'You're very famous, David. Did you know? There's a picture of you in this baseball magazine.'

He showed David and Midori the magazine. There was a picture of Patsy O'Hara, the star player of the New York Yankees. He was in Tokyo to coach the Yomiyuri Giants. There was also a picture of his son. His name was Patsy O'Hara junior. He looked exactly like David.

Later that evening, David watched baseball on TV with Midori's family.

'Do you like baseball, David?' Midori's father asked.

'Well...,' said David.

Midori's father laughed. 'You're an Englishman,' he said. 'I'm sure you prefer cricket.'

Midori wanted to show David the most famous sights near Fukuoka. First, they stayed in the city and visited the Asian-Pacific Exposition. The next day, they went to Mount Aso, an active volcano. After that, they went to Yanagawa, where the famous Japanese poet Hakusha Kitahara was born.

Like all visitors to Yanagawa, they went for a boat trip. Midori noticed another boat following them. There were three men in it, a Japanese and two Westerners.

Later, Midori saw the men in the car park. They got into a big red car. The car had American number plates.

Next, they went to a special hotel in Beppu. There were hot springs at Beppu. Midori told David to go and have a bath in the hot water.

'Be careful,' she said. 'The water's very hot. It's also very steamy inside. You can't see anything.'

Midori waited for David in reception. Suddenly she saw the red car again. The Japanese man was in the driver's seat. Then the two Westerners ran out of the hotel. They carried something heavy in a large towel. They put it into the car and drove away.

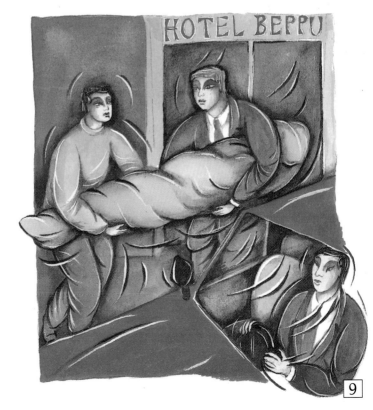

Midori ran to an attendant.

'Excuse me,' she said. 'Is the foreign boy still in the bathroom?'

The attendant went to check. He came back.

'No,' he said. 'I'm sorry. He's not there.'

Midori ran to a telephone. She called the police.

'Please help,' she said. 'I'm at Beppu. Three men took my friend David. Come quickly!'

Soon a police car arrived and two policemen got out.

'Why did the men take your friend?' one policeman asked.

'They thought he was Patsy O'Hara's son,' Midori told them. 'They took the wrong boy.'

The policemen didn't understand. Then Midori had an idea. She showed them her photo of David. Then she pointed to a magazine on a newsstand. It was a baseball magazine. On the cover of the magazine there was a photo of Patsy O'Hara and his son.

Midori described the three men and told the policemen the number of the American car. One of the policemen radioed the police station.

'Come on,' he said to Midori. 'The American car is going south-west along Route 57. I think they're going to Kumamoto Airport. We must hurry.'

Midori jumped into the police car and they drove off.

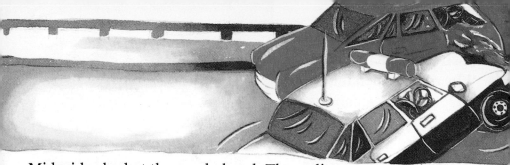

Midori looked at the road ahead. The police car was going very fast. She was excited, but she was very worried about David. Where was he? Was he all right?

The second policeman turned round. He smiled at her. 'Don't worry,' he said. 'Everything will be all right.'

Midori pointed at the road ahead of her.

'Look,' she said. There was the big American car.

The police car drove up beside it, but the American car didn't stop. Then the police driver turned the steering wheel suddenly and the American car ran off the road.

The driver of the American car was hurt. He didn't move. The two other men jumped out of the car and ran up the road to Kumamoto Castle. The policemen ran after them.

The two men tried to run into the castle but the policemen were too quick for them. One of the men pulled out a gun and fired. He missed. The first policeman dived at the man and knocked the gun out of his hand.

The second policeman picked up the gun and pointed it at the man. The man held up his hands. The policemen put handcuffs on the two men and led them back to the police car.

Midori helped David out of the back of the American car.

'Oh Midori,' David said. 'I'm so pleased to see you.'

The next day, David's father came from Tokyo. Midori's mother cooked a special meal. Everyone enjoyed it very much.

After dinner, the phone rang. Midori answered it.

'Hi,' an American voice said. 'This is Patsy O'Hara. The police told me all about your adventure. I want to thank you and David. I want to invite you and your families to the baseball game on Saturday.'

On Saturday evening, they all watched the game with the O'Hara family. David sat next to Patsy O'Hara junior. The two boys looked like twins. David couldn't believe it.

'Well, David,' said Midori's father. 'Is baseball as exciting as cricket?'

'I don't know about that,' he said. 'But it's certainly not as exciting as a hot springs bath!'

Heinemann International
A division of Heinemann Publishers (Oxford) Ltd
Halley Court, Jordan Hill, Oxford, OX2 8EJ

OXFORD   LONDON   EDINBURGH
MADRID   PARIS   ATHENS   BOLOGNA
MELBOURNE   SYDNEY   AUCKLAND   SINGAPORE   TOKYO
IBADAN   NAIROBI   GABORONE   HARARE
PORTSMOUTH(NH)

ISBN 0 435 27724 3

This reader is also available on cassette
ISBN 0 435 27833 9

© Tony Hopwood, 1991
First published 1991

Designed by Threefold
Illustrations by Sue Hillwood Harris

Typeset by Threefold Design
Printed and bound in Spain by Printeksa

HEINEMANN NEW WAVE READERS
Series Editor: Alan C. McLean
Level 2

Double Danger by Tony Hopwood
Karateka by Sue Leather and Marje Brash
Kate's Revenge by Philip Prowse
Zargon Zoo by Paul Shipton

92 93 94 95 96 10 9 8 7 6 5 4 3 2